REVIEW

OF THE

REPORT OF THE SENATE COMMITTEE

ON THE

RETURNS OF THE SEVENTH CENSUS.

WASHINGTON:
GIDEON AND CO., PRINTERS.
1852.

CENSUS OFFICE, *Washington, July* 5, 1852.

I deem it a duty to all concerned in the condensation of the United States statistical returns—to the Head of the Department to which this office is attached, and to the numerous assistant marshals throughout the United States, as well as to those who have manifested a deep interest in the progress of the work—to present some explanatory comments upon various portions of the report of the Committee of the Senate of the United States, presented June 28, 1852; and, in doing so, would disclaim all intentional disrespect to any member of the committee.

In the following pages the entire report will be found reprinted; and, that there may be no ground for the charge of misrepresentation, the reader will find the text and comment side by side.

My object is simply to rescue that portion of the Maryland census which comes within the requirements of the law, from the odium which must necessarily attach to it when with reference thereto the Committee speak of "the falsity of these pretended statistics," and I hope to show satisfactorily that the committee have fallen (doubtless unintentionally) into many errors in their statements, and given the high sanction of their opinion to conclusions formed on, perhaps a very natural, misconception, arising from the complicated nature of the subject, but which cannot be sustained when the grounds thereof are properly examined.

The authority of Congress demanded the preparation of one portion, and the other was freely presented for its acceptance or rejection, with no view to the advancement of any personal interests. For the publication of the latter, on the ground of merit, I express no wishes and offer no arguments. They are chapters, comprising simply a summary of statistical and physical facts, which will be of value to the statist and political economist, and cannot be affected by legislative decision, one way or another.

JOS. C. G. KENNEDY.

RETURNS OF THE SEVENTH CENSUS.

Mr. BAYARD, from the Select Committee to which the subject was referred, presented to the Senate the following report relating to the publication of the returns of the Seventh Census.

The Select Committee to whom was referred for revision the plan for the publication of the returns of the Census, as exemplified in relation to the State of Maryland, report: *

That, in the revision of the plan for the publication of the Census returns, submitted to the Senate by the Department of the Interior, the committee have not only examined the form in which the information is presented in relation to the State of Maryland, but have extended their *investigation* into the probable *correctness* and *reliability* of the *statistical returns.*

But one member of the Committee visited the office; where he spent five minutes in looking at one return. No returns were ever taken for examination by the Committee; so that it seems to me impossible for them to have investigated any returns except those "in the form in which the information is presented in relation to the State of Maryland."

If the actual statistical returns have not, either from the complicated inquiries to be made, the short period allowed for the performance of the service, or want of capacity or negligence on the part of the subordinate agents, a sufficient approximation to accuracy to render them reliable for any useful deduction, then it is manifest that their publication *as facts* should not be authorized by Congress.

No one could dissent from this proposition; and, if the facts shall be found such as to justify the premises, no objection could reasonably be urged to the conclusions arrived at; while, in the opinion of the writer, it will be made to appear that, in general, the returns are remarkably perfect. It was never designed to publish "as *facts*" the "*actual statistical returns.*" Congress could never authorize "their publication."

The most eligible and simplest mode in which objections, either to the form of publication proposed or the proximate accuracy of the facts returned, can be presented is by a revision of the plan of publication as exemplified in the "Census" of Maryland, in the order in which the subjects and tables are there stated.

The first objection is to the historical account of Maryland and its counties, embracing fifteen pages, from one to fourteen, both inclusive.

The committee are of opinion that a historical account should be excluded in reference to Maryland, as well as other States, as unauthorized by the act of Congress, and foreign to the statistical inquiries directed by it.

Does an act of Congress authorize (in advance) the preparation of every work published under its sanction? Does the publication of a

* The "Report" in small and the "Review" in large type.

RETURNS OF THE SEVENTH CENSUS.

Mr. Bayard, from the Select Committee to which the subject was referred, presented to the Senate the following report relating to the publication of the returns of the Seventh Census.

The Select Committee to whom was referred for revision the plan for the publication of the returns of the Census, as exemplified in relation to the State of Maryland, report: *

That, in the revision of the plan for the publication of the Census returns, submitted to the Senate by the Department of the Interior, the committee have not only examined the form in which the information is presented in relation to the State of Maryland, but have extended their *investigation* into the probable *correctness* and *reliability* of the *statistical returns.*

But one member of the Committee visited the office; where he spent five minutes in looking at one return. No returns were ever taken for examination by the Committee; so that it seems to me impossible for them to have investigated any returns except those "in the form in which the information is presented in relation to the State of Maryland."

If the actual statistical returns have not, either from the complicated inquiries to be made, the short period allowed for the performance of the service, or want of capacity or negligence on the part of the subordinate agents, a sufficient approximation to accuracy to render them reliable for any useful deduction, then it is manifest that their publication *as facts* should not be authorized by Congress.

No one could dissent from this proposition; and, if the facts shall be found such as to justify the premises, no objection could reasonably be urged to the conclusions arrived at; while, in the opinion of the writer, it will be made to appear that, in general, the returns are remarkably perfect. It was never designed to publish "as *facts*" the "*actual statistical returns.*" Congress could never authorize "their publication."

The most eligible and simplest mode in which objections, either to the form of publication proposed or the proximate accuracy of the facts returned, can be presented is by a revision of the plan of publication as exemplified in the "Census" of Maryland, in the order in which the subjects and tables are there stated.

The first objection is to the historical account of Maryland and its counties, embracing fifteen pages, from one to fourteen, both inclusive.

The committee are of opinion that a historical account should be excluded in reference to Maryland, as well as other States, as unauthorized by the act of Congress, and foreign to the statistical inquiries directed by it.

Does an act of Congress authorize (in advance) the preparation of every work published under its sanction? Does the publication of a

---

* The "Report" in small and the "Review" in large type.

geologists, with sufficient time for the thorough and accurate performance of this duty. Nor, in fact, does the subject appear to be appropriately connected with the returns of a decennial enumeration of the inhabitants, made under the provisions of the Constitution.

The Committee therefore recommend the omission of these geological sketches.

The persons engaged in the preparation of the geological portions *are* of "established reputation;" and are competent to the task, provided the geological sketch of Maryland is a good publication. The others will at least be equal to it. That presented, has obtained the highest complimentary testimony from the most distinguished authorities in this or any other country; and, if the work prepared secures the approbation of the highest authorities of "most established reputation," it will require some other reason to convince me that it is not worthy of adoption. A perusal of the chapter on the geology of Maryland will satisfy the reader that it is a subject intimately connected with, and important as elucidating the statistical returns. An opinion, expressed in writing, by Prof. Benjamin Silliman, LL. D., will be introduced hereafter.

The tabular statement at page twenty, showing the progress of population from 1790 to 1850, should be retained, but the previous tables at page nineteen should be omitted, as they are admitted to be drawn from materials " meagre and unsatisfactory," and therefore cannot be reliable.

Why should this table of population from 1790 to 1850 be retained? The law of Congress does not require it. The same reason for which they would exclude the historical portion (authority of Congress) should apply with equal force here. The materials though "meagre and unsatisfactory" ***to the statist,*** are more reliable than nearly all the statistics of the world *prior to the 19th century.*

The account of the population of Maryland, from pages nineteen to twenty-two, both inclusive, prefixed to the tabular statements of the returns, is objectionable, as being in part a mere repetition of facts which sufficiently appear in the tables; and also because it in part contains the deductions of the compiler from the facts stated, when the object of the Census and its publication should be given to facts alone, leaving the deductions drawn from those facts to be sustained by the authority of the individual, and their own intrinsic weight and propriety, without adding the sanction of the legislature to views or opinions which, when published, might not be approved.

An illustration of the latter objection may be found at page nineteen, in the following passage: "It does not appear that the introduction of the African race among the body of the population had any marked effect upon its progress." This may be essentially true, but it is merely an opinion, and one the correctness of which would probably be questioned by many.

Any remarks prefixed to the tabular statements should be explanatory merely of the tables and their headings, and to that extent they are requisite.

The article entitled "Population of the State of Maryland" is an analysis and summary of the facts stated in the tables covering the 14 following pages, some topics being left untouched for want of time. It is believed to be a useful and necessary part of the work. That it is in part a repetition of facts set forth in the tables, is true, but the facts are repeated in combinations and under new forms of statement which render them more intelligible to the general reader, and impress them forcibly upon his memory by presenting them in a more interesting and attractive style. The detailed report of the Census is designed for two classes of persons, namely, the body of citizens who wish to inform themselves in a general way, and without critical nicety, of the physical condition of their country, its population, wealth, property, and capabilities; and, secondly, that class who require to study all the facts collected, in their minutest development, as legislators, administrative officers, and men of science. The article in question is specially intended for the former, but may be perused with advantage by both. Upon looking at the particular citations made by the Committee from this article they would appear to indicate that their objections are not of a serious character, and that they are presented only because it was necessary to take specific exceptions to sustain a general censure. If it be proper to show in a brief space the "progress of population from 1790 to 1850," why should an equally concise statement of its progress during the preceding 156 years be expurged? The *law* gives no specific authority for either table; and as to the first, what is it considered by itself, but such a repetition of facts given in these returns and those of preceding Censuses, as has just incurred the censure of the Committee. The Census report states that the table of population of Maryland from 1634 to 1790 is made up "from such records as the annals of the province and State present." Now, it is true, that these materials are comparatively "meagre and unsatisfactory," but will any body, whose opinion is entitled to respect, assert that they do not deserve consideration, and that being the best which remain, they ought not to be rescued from obscurity and probable loss, and may not properly be applied to the purpose for which they are here used? It is not thought necessary to say a word in defence of the propriety of inserting the table which the Committee condemn, but the writer, differing from the Committee, suggests that the actual population at given periods, and the progress of the race in numbers, has been a subject of keen inquiry and disputation, with the historians of every country and every age, and that no part of the historian's duty has been more difficult. No historian of England, for example, has thought himself at liberty to omit some estimate of its population, or to comment upon the estimates of others at periods anterior to 1801, when the first census was taken, and no portion of their works is more frequently adverted to or consulted with greater interest.

Next in order come the tabular statements of population, covering from pages twenty to twenty-six, both inclusive.

To these there is no objection, except a slight alteration in the general heading of "Free Colored" to the fourth table, where the total population of whites and free blacks is included under it. With this alteration, the Committee recommend their publication in the form presented.

The tabular statements from pages twenty-seven to thirty, both inclusive, showing the places of nativity of the inhabitants, may be well reduced to two tables, giving the aggregates for the State, with the sex and color, similar to the table headed "Recapitulation," at page thirty-five.

Under the general heading "Population," and after the classified details of the whites and free colored, by ages and sexes, the total population of whites is placed in the way of recapitulation with the free persons of color. If the Committee would present the *form* for such "two tables" as it proposes, the Senate would easily decide this matter, and would not long hesitate to reverse this recommendation. The adoption of a table from verbal description is not safe; any table worthy adoption is easily made by one who understands its purposes, and readily filled with twenty or more illustrations. It might be well to see its practical operation.

No sufficient reason appears for the expansion of this species of information, by showing the place of birth of the persons residing on a particular day in each county of a State or each ward of a city.

The proportion of native and foreign born citizens in the whole State may be desirable, and also of those born out of the State but in the United States, but the utility of giving the proportions residing on a given day in each county and in each ward of a city, is not perceptible.

It was not the residence on a *particular day*, but on a particular day was set down their residence general; one day would not make a residence, but the residence was made applicable, for uniformity, to the 1st of June, *to comply with the law*. (See section 19.) The individual may have been in Europe temporarily on the day designated, while he was reported as residing in Maryland, for that was his *legal* residence. In a different portion of the report, the Committee recommend the "expansion" of the population returns, to towns, townships, hundreds, &c.

The tables as presented, also, do not distinguish the sex or color; and in the opinion of the Committee two tables showing the nativity of the inhabitants of the State, without reference to local residence, and giving the sex and color, should be substituted for the tables of nativity in the proposed plan. They could readily be included in one-fourth of the space which the proposed tables of nativity occupy.

The Committee recommend this alteration in these tables.

It would not much reduce the tables in extent to "show the nativity of the inhabitants of the State, * * * giving the sex and color," but very essentially destroy their value.

The table showing the deaf, dumb blind, insane, and idiotic, occupying from pages thirty-one to thirty-four, both inclusive, may be omitted as merely useless. All the information in them really valuable is contained in the "Recapitulation" at page thirty-five. There is no perceptible advantage in giving the local residence on a particular day of persons so afflicted. If the places of birth had been stated, a speculative mind might perhaps have attempted to draw inferences from the effect of climate or locality on the origin of such diseases; but the mere residence, perhaps temporary, of each of these unfortunate beings on a particular day, can be of no moment in a medical point of view, and affords no information worth publication for any available purpose.

I beg to differ with the Committee. The plan adopted furnishes facilities for institutions of beneficence to seek out the sufferers, which otherwise would not exist. This is the great use of the investigations respecting these unfortunate classes of individuals. The reasons given for the changes are speculative, while those for the table as it exists are humane and philosophic. It is as necessary to know the *residence* as the *birth-place*, to arrive at what the Committee suggests, while the limitation to accord with their recommendation, would be opposed by every officer of an asylum in the United States.

The table headed "Recapitulation," at page thirty-five, gives all that is desirable—the sex, the color, the free, and the slave, and also the place of birth, whether in the State, the United States, or a foreign country. It is an admirable condensation, and, compared with the previous extended tables for each county, is a strong illustration of the useful, as contradistinguished from the useless. The Committee thereforere commend the omission of these tables relating to the deaf, dumb, &c., except the "Recapitulation" at page thirty-five.

The Committee also recommend the omission of the table of "Manumitted and fugitive slaves," on the same page, believing that the sources of information make its accuracy questionable, whilst the utility of its publication, if accurate, is not obvious. No returns are given in this table from four counties, and the number of fugitives recovered does not appear.

Did not the law require the number of fugitives to be stated as well as the number manumitted? Had these tables been omitted, the work would have been censured as *not* containing what the act of Congress required. "No returns are given from four counties," because there were none manumitted, and no fugitives from these counties, and the law did not require the "number of fugitives recovered" to be given. Any who had been *recovered* could not have been at the time, fugitives from bondage.

No objections are apparent to the enumeration of the "professions, occupations, and trades," at page thirty-six, and its publication is recommended.

The "agricultural productions," comprised in four tables, cover pages thirty-seven and thirty-eight, and though with doubts as to the accuracy of the facts returned, arising from the manifest deficiencies in other statistical statements, the Committee having no means of testing their correctness, recommend their publication.

With the "doubts" expressed, it seems to me that *consistency* would have required a different opinion, if the argument that the publication by Congress necessarily implies that Congress endorses them "as facts" is to hold good.

Next in order come the "industrial establishments," which cover twenty-four pages, from pages thirty-nine to sixty-two, both inclusive. If this portion of the statistics is at all reliable, certainly the tables may be reduced in publication. Twelve pages, from thirty-nine to fifty-one, are devoted to tables showing the location in the twenty wards of the city of Baltimore of the different branches of industry, with the capital employed, &c.; and all this information is condensed, at pages fifty-two, fifty-three, into two tables for the whole city, which seems preferable. Only eight pages are devoted to the rest of the State. The advantage of this minuteness in the statement of the residence of persons pursuing different occupations in each ward of a city, is not believed to be commensurate with the increase it would cause in the size and cost of the publication, if indeed it is attended with any practical utility.

I have ever thought it might be well to publish this information by cities and counties, but did not feel authorized so to reduce it.

In the opinion of the committee, however, the statistical returns of the "industrial establishments" are altogether too defective and unreliable to justify their publication; and unless Congress are prepared to promulgate, under governmental sanction, as facts, returns which manifestly do not approximate to accuracy, the whole of these tables should be stricken out. The evidence of the defects in these returns exists upon the face of the tables themselves.

These tables profess to give, and the officers were instructed to collect, the numbers and kinds of the different "Industrial Establishments," wherever the establishment or individual produced articles of a gross value exceeding five hundred dollars annually.

The law does not so require; it should read "producing articles to the annual value of $500."

A very cursory examination of the tables will show that these returns are in this respect grossly defective, and do not give, even by approximation, a true statement of the industrial establishments of Maryland. There are certain occupations and trades which must of necessity exist to some extent in every county in each State; and yet from three counties in Maryland (Charles, Caroline, and Calvert) there is no industrial establishment returned producing over five hundred dollars in value. In fifteen of the twenty counties there is not a single carpenter whose products exceed that value. Of two hundred and thirty-four carpenters producing that value or upwards, there are eighteen in Anne Arundel, and but two in the richer and more populous county of Frederick, and only one in Baltimore county. In twelve counties there are no clothiers or tailors, and five, including Alleghany, have not a single blacksmith, and Washington county but one, whilst they exist in large relative numbers in other counties, where their services would be less requisite, and employment less extensive and remunerative. There are enumerated but three millwrights in the State, two in the city of Baltimore and one in Cecil county, whose products exceed five hundred dollars annually.

This is all negative. The Committee have been extensively corresponding to collect arguments respecting the work, and why not *prove omission?* There are but few tailors in the country who produce articles to the annual value of $500; much of their time is spent in *repairs*, as the manufactured article can now be purchased cheaper than made. So with blacksmiths, most of whom live by "repairs" mainly; equally applicable to millwrights. The Committee seem to think it singular that a county containing, as Anne Arundel does, a populous manufacturing town like Ellicott's mills, and a city, should contain 18 *carpenter establishments*, (for the returns do *not* make it appear that there are *any* particular "number of carpenters" in a county.) The Committee, in saying that there "is only one in Baltimore county," seem here to overlook the fact that Baltimore city, containing 205 establishments, is located in Baltimore county.

The law says, enumerate the establishments "*producing articles* to the annual value of $500." Does the journeyman carpenter *produce* articles to the amount of $500; do many of the country carpenters "produce articles" to this amount? They (mostly) till a portion of land, and make repairs on houses, barns, &c. This comment is made to show that to discredit the returns a selection is made of those interests which might be expected from their nature to exhibit inconsistencies if any existed; and admitting (as I do not) that the inferences drawn by the Committee are legitimate, with respect to these occupations which are acknowledged to be extreme cases, that should not condemn the more correct returns producing $32,000,000.

Such results are incredible as correct statements of facts, and can only be accounted for by a negligence of inquiry, which might perhaps have been anticipated from the minuteness of the information sought, the number of questions to be asked and answered, and the improbabilty that competent persons would undertake the duties to be performed for the compensation allowed. The office, too, of assistant marshal, being temporary and not lucrative was, of necessity, merely incidental to the ordinary pursuits of the individual. It is, in the opinion of the Committee, altogether impossible to reconcile the inequalities in the distribution of the various branches of industry in different counties on any ground but that of deficiency in the returns, whether applied to the foregoing or other industrial pursuits existing in every community. Nor can it be supposed that the gross annual value of the products of a large majority of those engaged as employers, either as carpenters, blacksmiths, or indeed in any other trade, would not exceed five hundred dollars. The cost of material, which is included in gross value, would generally equal one-third of the amount, and if the person engaged in the pursuit employed but a single hand, his mere subsistence would require a production exceeding five hundred dollars annually. A few illustrations render this questionless. At page 62, at the "Recapitulation for the State," but three millwrights are given as producing an annual value exceeding $500. They have a capital embarked in the business of $17,500, and their annual products equal $49,000 in value, employing forty-two hands at an average monthly cost of labor of $1,250. At page 36, in the "List of Professions, &c.," the returns show that there are one hundred and two millwrights in the State; and assuming these forty-two hands to be included in the whole number of millwrights, it is not rationally supposable that no one of the remaining fifty-seven produces property of a value exceeding $500 annually. The probability is that the products of a large majority exceed that amount.

Much of this seems very trifling, and is moreover, incorrect; the reare no number of millwrights enumerated at page 62. The *number of establishments* alone is given. Millwrights in Maryland do much in the way of *repairs*, while in 1850 but little was done in the way of *construction*. The Committee, evidently, do not exactly, comprehend the proper distinction between "establishments" and "workmen."

There does not appear to be a bookbinder, except nine in the city of Baltimore, whose products exceed $500 in value, and yet there are seventy-eight in the State.

Country bookbinding is generally a very small business, and as those in Baltimore produce $53,000 in work, it is not improbable that a majority of those cited are *workmen employed* by others. It is not anywhere stated that there *are but nine bookbinders* in Baltimore. The returns make 9 "*establishments*" in Baltimore, many, if not all, of which are partnership concerns. One establishment may have four partners, and twenty binders employed; these in the occupation abstract would count 24 bookbinders, although representing but "one establishment," or as the Committee would say "one bookbinder."

Two hundred and thirty-four carpenters and builders are enumerated in the whole State, at page 61, as producing each annually products exceeding $500 in value, of whom two hundred and five are located in the city of Baltimore, and eighteen in Anne Arundel county, leaving but eleven for the rest of the State. They employ one thousand two hundred and thirty-seven hands, and their annual products equal $1,518,117. At page 36 it is found that there are five thousand two hundred and forty-four carpenters and builders in the State, exclusive of one thousand two hundred and seventeen masons and bricklayers. Deducting the one thousand two hundred and thirty-seven hands and two hundred and thirty-four employers, there remain three thousand seven hundred and seventy-three carpenters, none of whom produce articles of an annual value over $500; and yet they must in part, if not a majority, be employers. The number would be still greater on the supposition that the masons and bricklayers are included among the hands employed by the carpenters and builders, which doubtless is the fact. This mode of investigation may be pursued as to almost any trade, and similar results will appear; yet Congress are asked to authenticate, by publication, such statements as giving *a true* account of the industrial establishments of Maryland.

The facts here stated, as to the number of carpenters and builders, will not be found on page 61, or any other page. If I say there is one "establishment," or firm, engaged on the masonry of the Capitol, does it follow that there is but one mason employed? The Committee confuse the facts connected with establishments, and the list of trades and professions. They select what may be well doubted as coming within the term manufacture, and respecting which the assistant marshals may have naturally entertained doubt; but it is a well known fact that the country is filled with men called carpenters, who give a portion of their time to other pursuits; and, admitting this statement to be true, it is not calculated to lessen the value of the returns, unless proof is adduced to show their incorrectness. It is presumed these *are* all of the number which legitimate reasoning would represent as not "producing articles" to the annual value of $500.

Another illustration of the falsity of these pretended statistics

Harsh expressions, when viewed in connexion with the fact that they are made to apply to the results obtained under the act of a previous Congress.

may be obtained by deducting the value of the raw material annually consumed, and the cost of labor from the gross annual value of the products as given in the tables. This is done on the assumption that the average monthly cost of labor, stated under the head of "wages," means the average monthly cost during the whole year. That this assumption is correct, appears not only from a fair construction of the schedules made part of the act of Congress, but also from the instructions given by the Department to the marshals and their assistants. Those instructions were printed for the use of the officers, and are very full and precise. On this subject the following directions appear at page 24 of the "Instructions:"

"Under the general heading, *hands employed,* is to be inserted, under *male and female column* 8 and 9, the *average* number of each sex employed *during the year* in the manufacture or business. These numbers are to be estimated either by an average of the whole year, or by selecting a day when about the average number was employed, and inserting the number on such day as the average.

"Under heading 10 and 11, entitled *wages,* is to be inserted the *average* monthly amount paid for all the labor of all the hands, male and female, employed in the business or manufacture *during the course of the year.*"

There is no room for misunderstanding here on the part of a man of ordinary intelligence; and, to explain or account for the discrepancies and absurdities in the returns which will be cited, on the supposition that *the monthly average cost of labor* does not include the average cost during the *whole* year, the explanation must be based on the presumption of a want of common intelligence or gross neglect on the part of the assistant marshals; and is at best (if the supposition be correct) a substitution of conjecture for fact, and equally impairs confidence in the accuracy of these returns. Those articles only are selected for illustration which most strikingly exhibit the incorrectness of the facts returned, though similar results are apparent in a less degree in many other branches of industry.

At page 64 two powder-mills are enumerated, having a capital of $64,000.

The value of the raw material consumed annually is stated at	$10,211
The monthly average cost of labor is $189—multiplied by 12 gives an annual cost of	2,268
Amount of raw material and labor	$12,479
The value of the annual products is	16,75
Less raw material and cost of labor	12,479
Leaves	4,271
Deduct the interest on capital	3,840
And there remains but	$431

With no allowance for wear and tear, the certainty of explosions, and contingencies.

Is it to be believed that such an illustration as this is brought to affect the character of the tables for credibility? What is the fact according to the record? It is, that the capital of $64,000 invested in "real and personal estate" in the business produces a revenue of $4,271, being equal to 6⅔ per cent. per annum, which is more of a dividend than is declared on the railroads in Massachusetts. Apply this argument to the iron works of Pennsylvania, and how will it work? This is one of the cases "which most strikingly exhibits the incorrectness of the facts returned." That powder making is not very profitable in Maryland may be inferred from the fact that the number of mills is greatly reduced within the last few years.

There is one soapstone manufactory in the State, located in the city of Baltimore, and at page 52 the following statement is found as to this occupation:

The capital invested in the business is........................		$100,000
The annual product is, in value............................		20,000
The raw material consumed................................	$8,000	
The cost of labor annually..................................	8,640	
		16,640
Leaving for interest, wear and tear, &c., on a capital of $100,000.............		$3,360

Now for this *soapstone* factory. It occupies a vacant square in the city of Baltimore, the value of which is included according to law, being part of the "*real estate* employed in the business;" also the quarry, the land of which is of intrinsic value after the removal of the stone. This real estate is probably enhancing in value at the rate of 6 per cent.; to analyze clearly, however, we find the raw material (stone) to be worth - - - - - - - - $8,000

Labor - - - - - - - 8,640

Equal to - - - - - - - $16,640

product amounts to $20,000, making profit of $3,360 on the labor and materials, and the wear and tear of a stone cutter's tools, (of soapstone not much.) The vacant lot is not injured. The profit is therefore 20 per cent., but the record is made to say what it does not say; the *annual* cost of labor is not given, and the statement *as given* is not found at page 52. It is admitted by the Committee that these are extreme cases.

There are enumerated at page 52 forty-five brick makers, having invested in their business a capital of $190,000.

The value of the raw material consumed annually is......................	$89,807
And whether fuel is included under this head does not appear.	
The average monthly wages are $25,424, equal for the year to...............	305,088
Making the cost of material and labor..................................	394,895
The value of annual products is..	332,550
Showing an annual loss of...	$62,345

A similar result appears as to this industrial pursuit throughout the State, though the loss is not quite so great.

Reference to the law, or the instructions referred to, would have convinced the Committee that it was unnecessary to intimate doubt respecting the "fuel" mentioned. All men know, too, that brick making establishments lie idle much of the time, and the table does not carry out the "annual cost of labor." Now, strike out three or four months for rainy or cold weather and repairs, and the dividend will not be a small one. It is evident that the manufacturer returned the "average monthly wages" (as required by law) as the average amount paid during the time the establishments were in operation. A brick maker would not make his calculations as if labor was employed the entire year.

At pages 52 and 61 one button maker is enumerated, with a capital of $1,000.

The value of raw material consumed	$2,500
The cost of labor $148, multiplied by 12, is	1,776
Making an aggregate cost of	4,276
The value of annual products deducted	2,340
Shows annually a loss of	$1,936

And raw material consumed of greater amount than its converted value. The errors in all these cases are not typographical, but in the returns.

As to the button maker, the Superintendent of Census in a letter to the chairman of this Committee admitted that this was evidently a mistake, and that $2,500 should be a much less amount *paid for bones.* This button maker found this occupation of so little profit that he shortly after abandoned it and left the State.

Seven cordage makers are enumerated at pages 52 and 61, with a capital of $28,500.

Their gross annual products are valued at the sum of		$106,600
The value of raw material is	71,430	
The cost of labor	31,008	
		102,438
Leaving		4,162

divisible among seven establishments, (one being worked by steam,) without any allowance for wear and tear, &c. But this branch of industry also shows that the raw material in the establishment located in the Seventh Ward of Baltimore bears the proportion of $50,300 in value to $65,000 of annual products, about four-fifths; and in the First Ward the raw material constitutes but two-fifths of the annual products. The average wages of the hands employed in this business in the same city are, in the First Ward, $33.33 per month, and in the Eighth Ward but $22 per month, both establishments working by hand.

It appears, also, that in the Seventeenth Ward the value of the raw material consumed is $12,000, the annual cost of labor $15,240; amounting together to $27,240; whilst the value of the annual products is $22,100; making an annual loss of $5,140.

Many of the workmen and much of the capital in a variety of manufactures are devoted to the matter of *repairing;* and this element, in a portion, forms the largest part of the income. The Committee predicate all their arguments upon the presumption that the return respecting the manufactured or formed articles embraces all the receipts of the workmen. The futility of such reasoning needs not to be insisted on.

In Baltimore there is also one bandbox-maker, who consumes raw material annually of the value of $225, pays wages to the amount of $1,260; amounting together to $1,485, and whose annual products are in value but $1,200. Instances might be multiplied, quite as glaring in the results, by pursuing the same mode of investigation through the statistics of the several counties as returned; but those which have been specified are believed to be sufficient for the purpose of showing the unreliable character of these returns as statements of facts or an approximation to facts.

In this case there is no return made, except for the *bonnet* boxes made; and, as in some other cases, the correction could not be made in time for the publication of the Maryland work.

It appears, also, that the occupation of "*butchers*," from not being returned with sufficient accuracy, has been entirely omitted; and yet this branch of industry, in which nearly nine hundred persons are engaged in Maryland, employs a large amount of capital, and the value of its products ought of necessity to enter into any correct statement of the productive industry of a State.

Does the butcher manufacture? Is a piece of beef a piece of handicraft—a piece of workmanship? What is the "*raw material*" of a saddle of mutton or a leg of pork? The butchers are returned among the trades and occupations, but not as *manufacturers*. We return all the stock of cattle on the 1st of June on farms, and the *value of animals slaughtered.*

The next table, at page 63, contains a statement of the "real and personal estate and taxes;" and this, it might have been supposed, would be less liable to error; but it exhibits on its face gross inaccuracy.

It is understood that the State tax in Maryland is uniform in all parts of the State, and dependent upon the valuation of real and personal estate in the different counties. The third column of the table gives the amount of the State tax in each county, and by comparing it with the first column, in which the valuation of the real and personal estate in each county is stated, the gross inequality in taxation, and palpable errors are apparent, and the instances are too numerous to admit the supposition that these errors are typographical. The tax in Anne Arundel on a valuation of $9,774,931 is $9,069, whilst that in Washington county, on a valuation of $1,499,231, is stated at $29,051. In Prince George's county the valuation is $11,711,254, and the tax but $6,053; and in Frederick county, on a valuation of $18,773,926, not double that of Prince George's, the tax is stated at $45,192, more than seven times as large; and similar, if not so great, discrepancies exist as to the details in other counties. The omissions also in the returns as to other taxes, such as road and poor, are so numerous as to destroy confidence in the table as a correct statement of the rate or amount of taxation in Maryland. The Committee cannot recommend the publication of this table.

The above is all typographical; and if the Committee had consulted with the head of the office, or invited him to consult with them, *they would have been made acquainted with the corrections.* Long before the Committee reported, we had corrected the $9,069 tax in Anne Arundel to $60,432, and the taxes of Prince George had been changed from $6,053 to $65,000. The taxable property in Washington county had been altered from $1,499,231 to $13,459,172.

The next table, on the same page, professes to give the rates of wages in the different counties of Maryland, and the returns from which it is compiled must have been founded on very loose estimates. It is palpably inaccurate. The average monthly wages of a farm hand, with board, in Calvert county is stated at $4 50, and in Queen Anne's at $8; yet the average daily wages of a day-laborer in Calvert are given at forty-four cents, and in Queen Anne's at twenty-five cents.

The daily wages of a carpenter in Somerset are stated in the fourth column at $1, and in the *adjoining* county of Dorcester at $1 75. This is manifestly impossible, as such a difference in value as an *average* rate of wages could not continue for a fortnight in adjoining counties.

This table is full of inaccuracies, and entirely worthless as a statement of facts. Its rejection is recommended.

It is presumed that $4 50 is the average price of monthly labor for farm hands, with board; slave labor of course is meant. The return is given as reported by the assistant marshal; he may have made an error in copying; he should, however, know the price of labor after visiting every family. The *requirements of the law*, in this particular, have been observed, and the "wages table" was inserted in the law *upon the urgent request of one of the members of that Committee* who criticise this table which "professes" to give the rates of wages, but which is now pronounced entirely worthless. The discrepancy in these two counties would not be likely to mislead the statist, as the Committee's work, is proof that the results given, carry with them the tests of their accuracy and the means of correction.

The succeeding table, at page 64, headed "pauperism and crime," appears to be incomplete, particularly in that part which relates to "crime." There are from seven counties no returns as to the number of persons convicted within the year or in prison on the 1st of June, A. D. 1850; and the returns are complete from but three counties out of twenty.

That portion which relates to pauperism appears less defective, but the Committee, wanting confidence in any portion of these returns, recommend its rejection.

The returns are believed to be correct from *all* the counties. The returns are omitted for no one county, and the table is in conformity with the requirements of the law.

The tabular statement headed "libraries" affords no evidence of error except the column which professes to give the "private libraries," which is manifestly inaccurate, and ought to be rejected. It cannot be credited that there are but twenty-one private libraries in the city of Baltimore, containing in the whole 43,400 volumes, and seventy-two private libraries in Alleghany county, containing 55,467 volumes. Omitting the statement of the private libraries, the Committee recommend the publication of the rest of this table.

The short table headed "newspapers and periodicals" is probably correct, and is unobjectionable in form, and its publication is recommended.

The accuracy of the eight tables, from pages 65 to 68, both inclusive, headed "education and churches," the Committee have no means of testing; and as the sources from which the information compiled in these tables was drawn would probably be less liable to error than the other statistical returns, the Committee recommend their publication.

The next tables in order, which are the last in the plan of publication as presented, are the medical statistics, to which are prefixed explanatory notes, and then follows an appendix, containing life tables for Maryland, based on the data contained in the returns. These tables, with their adjuncts, extend over thirty-six pages, from pages 69 to 104, both inclusive. It is a matter of regret to the Committee, though the attempt was made, that they were unable to obtain a scientific opinion from competent persons as to the accuracy of the returns embodied in these tables, and their real value and reliabilty.

As the Committee allege that they applied for information to scientific sources ineffectually, it might not be improper to inquire whether the information was *solicited in the name of the Committee?* I have been assured that the member who solicited the information did so so unofficially that on that account replies were withheld.

Independently, however, of the improbability that scientific inquiries of this character would or could be prosecuted correctly by persons not peculiarly qualified, the Committee find on the face of the tables sufficient evidence of the doubtful accuracy of the facts returned to require that the publication of these tables should not be recommended.

It is believed that accurate returns of past *unrecorded* events relating to births, marriages, and deaths could, under no circumstances, be expected, and that little reliance in any mode in which they might be collected would be placed upon them by the statist; but, when the persons making the inquiries have no peculiar compentency or knowledge to qualify them for the duty, and the inquiries are in general addressed (in connexion, too, with numerous and complicated questions as to distinct matters) to those ignorant of the importance of accurate answers, even a remote approximation to accuracy cannot rationally be anticipated.

With reference to the "competency or knowledge" to qualify the assistants "for the duty," their competency has nothing whatever to do with the matter. *They* give no name to disease; they simply propose the questions according to the instructions given, and record the answers as returned by the head of the family. Would not the parent have in his *heart* a "record" of the death of his child, if it occurred within the year, and would not the child recollect that of the parent? So with husband and wife, master and slave. I think a man of ordinary feelings could recollect the death of one of his *horses*. It may therefore be premised, with respect to the argument in this paragraph, that no "head of a family" could be presumed so ignorant as to be unable to answer correctly the question, "has a death occurred in this family within the year past?" This admitted, we get at the *number* of deaths. Can the "head of a family" be supposed to know accurately the "sex?" If so, we arrive at another important fact. Would he probably be able to tell whether the decedent was a negro or a white person? If so, another element is obtained; would he be able to tell the age?—obituary notices generally do, and it is apt to be a fact recorded by the family. Now, lastly, as to the disease: cannot it generally be told if a person dies of small-pox, whooping-cough, measles, scarlatina, &c.; and is not the cause of death usually remembered for a twelve-month? It therefore seems to me that, in the nature of things, statistics of mortality are more to be relied on when obtained in this way, than in almost any other, and can be given with much more certainty than can the bushels of potatoes, turnips, and buckwheat, or the pounds of butter and cheese of the farmer, the publication of which returns is recommended.

Some evidences of the improbability of the facts as presented by these medical statistics are adduced, though doubtless a scientific physician could readily enlarge the list of errors, so as to destroy all confidence in their correctness or reliability.

The classification of causes of mortality is a deplorable jumble of technical names of diseases with those which are ordinarily used by the unlearned portion of the community; and in many cases the only description of the diseases causing death is the designation of the organ which they appeared to affect.

Among the enumerated causes of death, at page 21, are "apoplexy," "diseases of the brain," and "diseases of the head;" "bronchitis," "cramp," and "diseases of the throat;" "consumption," "pneumonia," and "diseases of the lungs;" "gravel," "diabetes," and "diseases of the kidneys;" "diarrhœa," "dysentery," and "diseases of the bowels." Diseases of the heart, of the spine, and of the stomach, are also among the indefinite descriptions used; and the table closes at page 72 with giving "unknown" as the cause of more than *one-fourth* of the deaths.

The language of the Committee with reference to the medical statistics, is perhaps the strongest used in their report, which terms "the classification of causes of mortality a *deplorable jumble*," &c., &c. That an honest conviction of reality of the charge was entertained, cannot be doubted, as the Committee enumerate seventeen *illustrations*, selected from the nomenclature of diseases in the Maryland census which appear above. It can be most easily shown, however, that even those selected to illustrate the truth of the assertion of the Committee are used in these medical statistics upon authority not easily set at naught, and have sufficient endorsement not only to justify their use and screen them from meriting the opprobrious epithets bestowed thereon, but sufficient to prove that they are in themselves proper, and that their omission would have effected a serious blemish in the medical tables. The National Medical Convention of the U. S. adopted a report, in 1847, containing a nomenclature and classification of *causes of death*. (See Sanitary Report of Mass., 1850, page 150.) This nomenclature has been adopted by the Medical Board of Health of Mass.; and prefatory to its introduction in the "appendix to the sanitary report for 1850," (page 391,) the following words are used, viz:

"The following alphabetical nomenclature of the principal fatal diseases and causes of death, contains the terms *which we recommend* to be used in the registers." Such authority for a nomenclature, with such an endorsement, we deem pretty safe, and will apply it to those cases which the Committee signalize with such severity. We will take the cases in the order in which they are quoted by the Committee, prefacing each with the numerical sign in the sanitary report. 31st on the list stands apoplexy; 41, disease of the brain; 46, bronchitis; 47, consumption: 51, pneumonia; 52, disease of the lungs; 74, gravel; 73, diabetes; 75, disease of the kindeys; 4, diarrhœa; 5, dysentery; 54, disease of the bowels; 44, disease of the heart; 85, disease of the spine; 63, disease of the stomach; so that of the 18 diseases cited, no less than 15 of the same are to be found in this table, and the other three will be found in the medical tables adopted by Dr. Barton in his Louisiana medical reports. In the "Registrar's" medical report for the city of Boston for the year 1850, will be found the following diseases occasioning death: Apoplexy, diseases of the brain, bronchitis, cramp, diseases of the throat, consumption, diseases of the lungs, diabetes, disease of the kidneys, diarrhœa, dysentery, diseases of the bowels, disease of the heart, disease of the spine, disease of the stomach.

These are all cited by the Committee. Had cases of death occurred to warrant it, the other names in use would have been included with them. The board of health for Baltimore includes in its table of mortality for 1851 the following diseases, viz: Apoplexy, inflammation of the brain, bronchitis, consumption, diabetes, diarrhœa, dysentery, inflammation of the bowels, spinal affection, &c. Thus it is with all modern and well accepted medical nomenclature, and a reference to the reports of the medical board of Washington, if referred to, would have saved the necessity of picking out the diseases cited to throw discredit on the medical statistics. The aim of men of real learning is to do away with all that *affectation* of science which cannot brook simplicity, and therefore in the medical report of Massachusetts, after giving directions for the names of diseases, the board continues, "according to this rule *consumption* is to be preferred to phthisis pulmonaris, pneumonia to inflammation of the lungs," &c., citing for illustration some of the *very cases* to which the Committee excepts.

If this should not be deemed sufficient, attention is asked to the opinion given by the high medical and scientific authority in the following letter:

WASHINGTON, D. C., *May* 17, 1852.

J. C. G. KENNEDY, esq., *Supt. of Census.*

MY DEAR SIR: I thank you for the copy of your valuable history and statistics of the State of Maryland, which you were so good as to send me day before yesterday, with a request that I should examine the tables of medical statistics, and give you my opinion concerning the plan adopted for the arrangement.

I have great pleasure in stating my profound conviction that you have adopted the very best method of showing at a glance the relative mortality of the different parts of the country, and of the relative predominance of certain diseases in different places. Such tables are most highly valued by physicians and by the officers of life insurance offices, and in Europe you may feel fully satisfied your labors will be gratefully appreciated, as they will be here by all enlightened physicians. I am glad to find you have adopted the alphabetical arrangement which affords so much convenience in reference, and which will enable any one to re-arrange and classify the particular diseases he may wish to compare and investigate.

This method has the advantage of being free from hypothesis, and is the one always preferred in the imperfect and advancing sciences like that of medicine.

I was also very much pleased with the plan of making colored statistical charts of the diseases prevalent in different States of the Union, and think that when your whole system of tabulated medical statistics is completed, that this method will be found practicable, but the tabular work must serve as a guide in the formation of such maps.

Trusting that you will receive the support of all enlightened men, and that you will receive aid from many of our medical societies—

I have the honor of offering you my personal sympathy, and of subscribing myself

Your obedient servant,

CHARLES T. JACKSON, *M. D.*,

Member of the Mass. Medical society; of the American Academy of arts and sciences; of the Geological society of France; vice prest. Boston society of Natural history; Assayer to the State of Mass. and of the city of Boston, Chevalier de la legion d'honneur, &c., &c., &c.

Thus much for *American* authority in defence of the nomenclature. On turning to the 8th and 9th reports of the registrar general of Great Britain, page 90, 94, we will find the British nomenclature as applied to the deaths in London for the years 1847, 1848. Included in that list will be found, No. 33, apoplexy; 41, disease of the brain; 44, bronchitis; 46, pneumonia; 50, disease of the lungs; 75, diabetes; 79, disease of the kidneys; 7, diarrhœa; 8, dysentery; 53, disease of the heart; 67, disease of the stomach." After quoting such authorities for the nomenclature used in the Maryland work, it is unnecessary to argue its correctness. The authorities, while they sustain the work, prove that real science can adapt itself to the simplest terms, and that what some might term the deformity of the census of Maryland, is its chief ornament. Respecting the complaint that one fourth of the deaths are returned as "unknown." To show that such return is not unprecedented, it will be seen by referring to the table of mortality from the official returns of St. Louis, that precisely the same proportion are returned "unknown;" and in addition to this no less than two fifths of those returned as "unknown" in the Maryland table, are of those dying in infancy.

The population in Caroline county is 8,884, and that of the adjoining county of Queen Anne's 10,214. The deaths in Caroline are reported at 71 for the year, and in Queen Anne's 238—consumption being the prevailing disease in both counties. The proportion is nearly three to one, which, though possible, seems improbable. In Somerset, with a population of not quite double that of Caroline, the deaths are 389; more in proportion than two to one. In Worcester, adjoining Somerset, with nearly an equal population, the deaths are but 192, or about one-half. In Talbot, with but 9,677 inhabitants, the deaths are 168, double those in Caroline, and nearly equal to those in Worcester.

These counties all have a similar climate and similar habits and modes of living among the people, and the difference in mortality seems incredible, unless well authenticated.

In the mountainous region similar differences appear. Alleghany, with a population of 22,045, has 149 deaths reported; and in Washington, with a population but one-third greater, there are 335 deaths. In Frederick county, with a population of 31,466, exclusive of the city, the deaths are 426, nearly doubling the proportionate mortality in Alleghany. A more striking illustration will be found, however, at page 93, in table 1 of these statistics, of the utter improbability of the truth or accuracy of the facts returned. In Queen Anne's the births are stated to be 320, and the deaths in the first year 59; whilst in Dorchester, with 410 births, there are but three deaths in the first year; the prevalent disease in both counties being consumption.

Apart from the disproportion between the counties, it is believed that the small number of deaths in Dorchester in the first year, in proportion to births, is incredible, and against all experience.

In the opinion of the Committee, these medical statistics are unfit for publication.

The population of the several counties enumerated above embraces only the *free* persons. The whole population of Caroline county is 9,962, and the whole number of deaths 76, of which the 71 stated are free.

The whole population of Queen Anne's is 14,484, and the whole number of deaths 324; of which the 238 stated are of free persons.

The whole population of Somerset is considerably *more* than double that of Caroline, being 22,456, and the whole number of deaths 526; of which 389 are of free persons, the figure 2 in the last number being a typographical error. The great difference in the mortality of these two counties, as reported in the marshals' returns, may possibly arise in part from error; but much of it is no doubt attributable to natural causes. Somerset is bounded on two sides by the Chesapeake Bay, and on a third by the Nanticoke river, while Caroline is situated in the healthiest part of the Eastern Shore, having for its eastern boundary the State of Delaware. Besides this, Somerset comprises one of the largest towns on the Eastern Shore.

The whole population of Worcester is 18,859, and the number of deaths 246; of which the 192 stated are of free persons. Though this county adjoins Somerset, its whole eastern boundary is the Atlantic ocean; and it is a well known fact that the shores of the ocean are subject to fewer diseases, and are in every respect more salubrious than the shores of bays, rivers, and creeks. The difference in the number of deaths, therefore, in these two counties, may be very well attributed to natural causes.

The whole population of Talbot is 13,811, and the whole number of deaths 240; of which the 168 stated are of free persons. The difference between the number of deaths in this county and in Caroline may also be accounted for, in great measure, without supposing the existence of error. Talbot borders on the Chesapeake Bay, and is indented by numerous inlets and arms of the bay, which tend to make it unhealthy. It contains, also, the town of Easton.

The difference in the deaths of Alleghany and Washington counties may perhaps be explained by the fact, that the large and populous town of Hagerstown is situated within the latter county; and it is known that the proportion of deaths to the population is always greater in large cities and towns than in the country. There may also be, and probably are, errors in the returns.

The same remark will apply to Frederick county, in which are embraced several populous precincts of the city of Frederick.

With regard to the proportion of deaths in the first year, to the whole number of deaths in the two counties of Queen Anne's and Dorchester, even after correcting the typographical errors of the printed returns, it must be admitted there is good reason to believe that the marshals' returns were, to an unusual degree, inaccurate; the deaths in the first year in Queen Anne's should be 73 instead of 71, and there are four deaths of *ages unknown*, all of which, it is possible, may have occurred within the first year. In Dorchester the number should have been 10 instead of 3. Respecting this county I am free to admit that the returns were inaccurate; but admitting inaccuracy in a portion, does not destroy the value of all, and as this is the first effort ever made to procure these important statistics, it is hoped that Congress will not require them to be perfect to ensure their publication. Dr. Barton, of Louisiana, a medical author of reputation, has deemed these statistics of sufficient value to found upon them elaborately executed maps of four of the States with which he is most familiar—a fact exhibiting the strongest possible proof, of their practical utility.

The use of tables founded on such unsatisfactory data should of course be rejected; but they are liable to the further objection of not coming within the authority entrusted by the act of Congress, and seem altogether out of place.

The Committee is certainly much in error as to what is and what is not to be viewed as coming within the law of 23d May, 1850. Senators will find a copy of the table for collecting the statistics of mortality at page 436, 31st Congress, Little & Brown's edition.

It is scarcely to be doubted that the scientific world would place but little reliance on life tables computed from a decennial enumeration of unrecorded events, made by unskilful persons, and founded on the mere memories and careless answers of individuals, many exceedingly ignorant, and most unaware of the necessity of extreme accuracy in their replies.

On this subject it seems to me that already is the proof sufficient to lead to a different opinion; and a careful analysis of the life tables formed for Maryland, and a comparison thereof with those of other countries, will satisfy every impartial observer competent to decide, that the results afford great internal proofs of the correctness of these returns in the aggregate. See opinion of Dr. Mitchell, (annexed.)

This subject of medical statistics closes the plan submitted to the Senate for the publication of the Census. Having stated the objections to such parts of the returns as the Committee believed to be too unreliable for publication, there remains to be noticed a single omission in the tables which ought to be supplied. It is understood that in Maryland there are no local subdivisions less than counties, in which the population appears on the face of the returns, but that this defect does not exist in the returns from most of the other States. The Committee, therefore, recommend the construction and publication of tables, showing the population alone in the local subdivisions of States less than counties, such as towns, townships, hundreds, &c., wherever the returns are sufficient for their formation. Such tables would occupy but a small additional space, and would often be of advantage in the legislative arrangement of election districts, and for other purposes. In recommending the rejection of so large a portion of the returns, founded on the inaccuracies apparent in the Census of Maryland as presented, the recommendation is of course extended to all the States; for, though it is not improbable that in some States the returns may be more accurate, yet the presumption is reasonable that in others they might be less so, and that in general the returns from Maryland would be as accurate as those from other States; for the same general causes which have produced the errors and deficiencies in the Maryland returns, exist equally throughout the Union. The Committee also recommend that the condensed tables for the United States shall conform to the alterations suggested in the detailed tables for the States; for, though in an aggregate statement of the industrial establishments of the Union the errors might not be apparent, they would exist, and the publication be not only useless but injurious, as the details from which the aggregate tabular statements must be made are found upon examination to be grossly defective and unreliable; and although it often happens that false deductions are drawn from correct statistics, yet certainly defective and inaccurate data can only lead to erroneous conclusions.

As it has been shown how unreliable are the premises upon which the foregoing recommendations are made, it is unnecessary to argue to a body, of such high intelligence as the United States Senate, how valueless must be the deductions.

The recommendation of the Committee, if adopted, will reduce the size of the publication somewhat more than four-fifths, and the expense of publication in proportion. In no case, however, have they been governed by the question of expense in the reductions they have recommended, though the cost of publication of a mass of useless or erroneous matter ought not to be disregarded.

Now, so far as the matter of expense is concerned, Congress may rest assured that the Census, on the plan proposed in the Maryland work, can be executed at a cost no greater than attended the publication of the Census of 1840; but that there may be no misapprehension on this matter, it is asserted that of the Census, on the plan proposed in the Maryland work, complete, 25,000 copies of two volumes each, or 50,000 volumes stereotyped and bound, can be furnished for $180,000, and of the consideration not one dollar asked until the work shall have been approved by a Congressional committee appointed for its examination; and for this bonds will be entered into for the sum named. The Committee propose so to reduce the work as shall diminish the cost "somewhat more than four-fifths," a saving which they contend will follow the adoption of their proposition. If so, the publication of the 7th Census must not cost $36,000, hardly one-fifth of the cost ten years ago.

Having reviewed the particular points of exception taken to the Maryland Census, and having shown that a majority of the errors noted in the tables of manufactures are mainly accidental, and not to be attributed to defect in the original returns, or necessarily incidental to the plan of their arrangement, and having satisfactorily shown that what is termed the "deplorable jumble" of medical returns, in place of being so is shown to be not only in accordance with propriety, but in harmony with the examples furnished and opinions given by the highest medical authority in this or any other country, I presume it will not be necessary to consider these questions further. Errors must exist in such a work, and much is effected when the errors carry with them the means for their detection. Every Census of the United States contains numerous errors, as many in the population returns as elsewhere, but on this account it has never been concluded that these returns are useless. In the absence of better data they afford an approximation of great value, and the results they exhibit are treated as matters of verity. Such, in their aggregates, they are, while in many of their details they may be grossly defective; thus it is with the inconsistencies in the returns cited by the Senate committee. Out of near *four thousand* manufacturing establishments, which produce more than thirty-two millions of dollars annually in value, half a dozen cases, admitted the most erroneous, are cited and upon an alleged discrepancy in the results presented by those selected, it is gravely recommended to omit all the returns of productive industry. Apply such reasoning to society, legislation, and laws, and what would become of us? Errors to ten-fold the amount here involved have been known to occur in the deliberately prepared speech of a member of Congress, and a long time has elapsed before correction. In searching for pebbles we overlook pearls.

The attention of Senators is solicited to the following letters:

SENATE CHAMBER, ANNAPOLIS, *March* 25, 1852.

J. C. G. KENNEDY, esq.

DEAR SIR: I have the pleasure to acknowledge the receipt of the two copies of the Census, including therein the history and statistics of Maryland. I gave one of the copies to a most intelligent gentleman, now a member of the Senate, and formerly Governor of our State, WILLIAM GRAYSON, of Queen Anne county. He is extremely gratified with it.

I have studied it diligently, and am every day more and more instructed and enlightened by its copious and interesting information, as well as exceedingly engaged with it.

I beg leave to return you my hearty thanks for it, and for the obliging manner in which you have bestowed it.

Respectfully, your obedient servant,
NATHANIEL WILLIAMS.

WOODSTOCK, CONN., *May* 7, 1852.

Mr. KENNEDY.

DEAR SIR: I have found time during a visit here to read the text of your work on Maryland, and to look over the tables.

I am much impressed with the value of your researches, and quite amazed at the amount of labor they must involve for you and your assistants. It appears to me, that if the plan is carried out for the United States, it must present very valuable results, and I hope and trust it will be adopted. In a document for the whole country, the historical part might and necessarily would swell to an inconvenient size, and might therefore be omitted, provided it would add too much to size and cost. The same remark will apply in a less degree to the geological portion, which is indeed interesting and valuable, and has of course a bearing upon the statistics of health, and life, and death.

Yours, truly,
B. SILLIMAN.

The French Minister of Public Works writing from Paris under date 29th of March, says:

"I thank you for the Maryland Census that I find drawn up in a complete and scientific manner, which throws new light on your country so little known in Europe. I hope Congress will adopt entire your plan, and will not think as an objection to the publication of what I may call a national work, the expense of some thousands of dollars more."

NEW ORLEANS, *April* 27, 1852.

MY DEAR SIR: I have just finished the task, the materials for which were so kindly furnished me by you, for which be pleased again to accept my sincere acknowledgments.

I am of opinion you are greatly mistaken in supposing you will have to look to posterity alone for credit, for the great work you are now laboring to accomplish. It is second to none in importance, undertaken by our, or indeed any other country, and will erect a lasting monument to your reputation, and be more appreciated just as it is understood.

Out of the medical returns, I have constructed a Sanitary Map for each of the States of Louisiana, Mississippi, Arkansas and Texas, to accompany and illustrate my report to the American Medical Association, meeting in Richmond, the first Monday in May. I beg you to accept a copy of each of these maps, in consideration of the favor you have done me. The only explanation required, probably is, that as it was impossible to express on one series of maps, the diversified sanitary condition arising from the greater or less prevalence of every form of morbid action, I have selected that class which embraces the mass of those maladies which constitute the distinction between healthy and sickly communities, so as to compare one country, State, or county, with another, and which are more or less under the control of police regulations and sanitary laws; the Zymotic (including fevers, cholera, intestinal diseases, &c.)

I have arranged them, as per marginal explanation, according to the number per thousand of the population which have suffered from them.

You see Louisiana has there a distinguished showing; this was owing to the great prevalence of cholera, (25 per cent. of the entire mortality having been caused by that disease.) You see how it followed the water courses, and the great routes of human intercourse, and how free the sea coast and pine woods were from it.

I wish the whole country was thus delineated; your labors would be then appreciated, and we should be enabled the more easily to compare the next census—showing, with this, to see how our countrymen may have been benefitted by the lesson; for, as I said above, these diseases arise in the main from *preventible conditions*, such as an advanced civilization should correct; and, to use the language of Dr. Rush, such as should be enforced by a *penalty!*

I have added some tables comparing the rural districts of my four States with the rural districts of Cuba, and the cities of Havana, Mexico, &c., from details I collected while travelling in those countries when in the army. They are curious, and highly in our favor.

I have also added all the meteorological details I could procure of the States assigned to me, and particularly of my State, and have added the *average solar radiation* for each month in the year.

It would be agreeable to me if these maps were shown to the delegation of my State.

I remain, with high regard,

Very respectfully, your obedient servant,

G. H. BARTON, M. D.

From J. K. Mitchell, M. D.

PHILADELPHIA, *July*, 1852.

J. C. G. KENNEDY, esq.

MY DEAR SIR: The two copies of the Maryland statistics sent to

Richmond were not received by me whilst in that city, and have been only now returned to me thence; where they have lain since May, I cannot tell. The other copy so kindly sent to me personally I shall have great pleasure and profit by retaining. The two designed for the Medical Association of the United States cannot be presented until next May at New York.

I would have immediately answered your polite note, but wished previously to examine your very elaborate work That having now done, I am delighted to find such a mighty mass of important knowledge so skilfully arranged and digested. Useful to every one; it will be inestimable to political economists and physicians. I assure you that, both as a mediciner and director of a Life office, (the old Pennsylvania company,) I have a full sense of the importance, as well as the ability, of your labors, and only hope that your health, and a necessary liberality in Congress, will enable you to give us not only such a work as that of Maryland upon each State, but that you will put your strong head and hand to a digest cf the whole, in which we may see at a glance the mighty interests and vital truths of the whole country. I am almost restless under the expectation of the completion of your labors, for which I really long.

I hope that Congress will enable you to expedite matters, and put no impediment in the way of the completion of what will do honor to the country, by showing the mighty resources, the vast strength, rapid progress, and good health of the Union. I wish to see you make an abstract which will bear the motto E PLURIBUS UNUM.

With many thanks for your kind recollection of me,

I have the honor to be,

Very truly and respectfully,

J. K. MITCHELL, *M. D.*

Prof. Lieber, LL. D, in a letter dated Columbia, S. C., 23d February, 1852, uses the following language : "And now, about your Maryland. The more I examine it the more I am gratified with it; and I begin to feel sure that, like all truly good and great works, it will show its excellence in the same degree as strict examination penetrates it."

REPORT OF THE MARYLAND HISTORICAL SOCIETY.

The following is the Report of the Committee appointed by the Maryland Historical Society at the meeting of February 13, 1852, to examine and report upon the Census returns for the State of Maryland:

The undersigned, to whom was referred the volume embodying the census returns for the State of Maryland, prepared by Jos. C. G. Kennedy, esq., one of the corresponding members of this society, and Superintendent of Census, respectfully report :

That while they are necessarily incompetent to express any opinion as to the correctness of the great mass of statistical information embraced in the volume referred to them, they discover no inaccuracies in those portions of the work which are of a historical and general character; and they consider the correctness of its statements in other particulars to be fairly presumable from the means afforded for the collection of information by the act of Congress, the pursuance of a well digested and comprehensive system of investigation under the direction of the able Secretary of the Interior, and the personal supervision of the intelligent statist at the head of the Census bureau.

The collection of facts so infinite in number, and varied in character, no matter how carefully and industriously made, can hardly, in the nature of things, be free from occasional inaccuracy; but your Committee do not doubt, from their knowledge of the care with which these returns have been collected, and the system of checks adopted by Mr. Kennedy to test their correctness, that this interesting statement of the population, resources, and present condition of the State, is as reliable as such returns can, under any circumstances, be made.

The State of Maryland has been selected by Mr. Kennedy for the development of the plan, in accordance with which he proposes, with the assent of Congress, to make up the returns for the whole country; and, as this plan is in many respects novel, your Committee have noted, with approbation, the points in which it chiefly differs from antecedent Census reports. The usefulness of such returns requires that they should be prepared so as to be bound up in volumes of convenient size; that the paper should be good, the type clear, and the arrangement of matter made with a view rather to facility of reference and comprehension, than to a misplaced economy of paper. In these respects the plan of Mr. Kennedy is certainly preferable to the old system, as, under it, the Seventh Census will be comprised in two volumes of the size and appearance of the American Archives, the one containing the tables of statistics of the entire country, and the other the historical, geographical, and other facts connected therewith.

Another noticeable contrast to the old plan is presented in a general prefatory sketch of the most important events connected with the history of the State from its first settlement; an account of each separate county, its physical features, minerals, streams, timber, water, and adaptation, naturally and artificially, to the purposes of manufactures and commerce; in a general geological account of the State; in a statement of its progress in population from the first to the present Census inclusive; in a review of its character for the health and longevity of its inhabitants; with tables presenting a history of the statistics of disease and mortality; calculations of the value of life among the several classes of its inhabitants; and in a large number of new subjects embraced in the statistical details; and in the manner of classification, which admit of the extraction of all the essential facts respecting the raw materials of each variety of manufactures, together with other features in which the statist will perceive important variations from any previous Census.

Your Committee do not consider it necessary to indulge in any remarks upon the propriety and necessity of these decennial reviews of the resources and progress of the country. Their great value has long since been recognised by the leading nations of Europe, and the practice of our own Government for seventy years past; but they do not think it inappropriate to express the hope that Congress will sanction in the plan of the report, upon which they are about to act, any changes calculated to develop more fully the striking facts of a history, growth, and condition unparalleled in national records, and the diffused knowledge of which would exert a most salutary influence upon our own people, and induce a juster appreciation of the character and strength of our country among the nations of the world.

The interesting statement of the number and services of the troops contributed by Maryland to the battle fields of the Revolution, has suggested the idea to your Committee, which they respectfully submit to Mr. Kennedy, whether a similar statement of the number of volunteers furnshed to the General Government by the several States, in the late war with Mexico—the great national event of the past lustrum—might not be developed into an interesting addition to his historical summary of the different States; as such facts, important as illustrating the character and strength of the people, would then be presented in a reliable and authoritative statement.

J. MORRISON HARRIS,
CHAS. F. MAYER,
JOHN H. B. LATROBE.

February 20, 1852.

www.ingramcontent.com/pod-product-compliance
Lightning Source LLC
LaVergne TN
LVHW011141110826
845150LV00008B/2458

* 9 7 8 1 4 1 8 1 9 3 2 3 2 *